Egyptian Prince

Contents

Introduction	5
The River Kingdom	6
Food and Drink	8
Palaces for Pharaohs	10
Going to School	12
Gods and Religion	14
Markets	16
Child of the Gods	18
Tombs and Treasures	20
Mummies	22
Life after Death	24
Timechart	26
Word List	28
Index	30
More Information	31

Designed and Produced by David Salariya

Editor	Shirley Willis
Design Assistant	Carol Attwood
Consultant	Henrietta McCall

Copyright © The Salariya Book Company 1992

All rights reserved. No part of this publication may be reproduced or transmitted, in any form or by any means, without permission.

First published in 1992 by
PAN MACMILLAN CHILDREN'S BOOKS
A division of Pan Macmillan Limited
Cavaye Place London SW10 9PG

ISBN 0-333-55640-2 (Macmillan hardback)
ISBN 0-330-32480-2 (Piccolo paperback)

A CIP catalogue record for this book is available from the British Library
Typesetting by C.S.T. (Hove) Ltd
Printed in Hong Kong

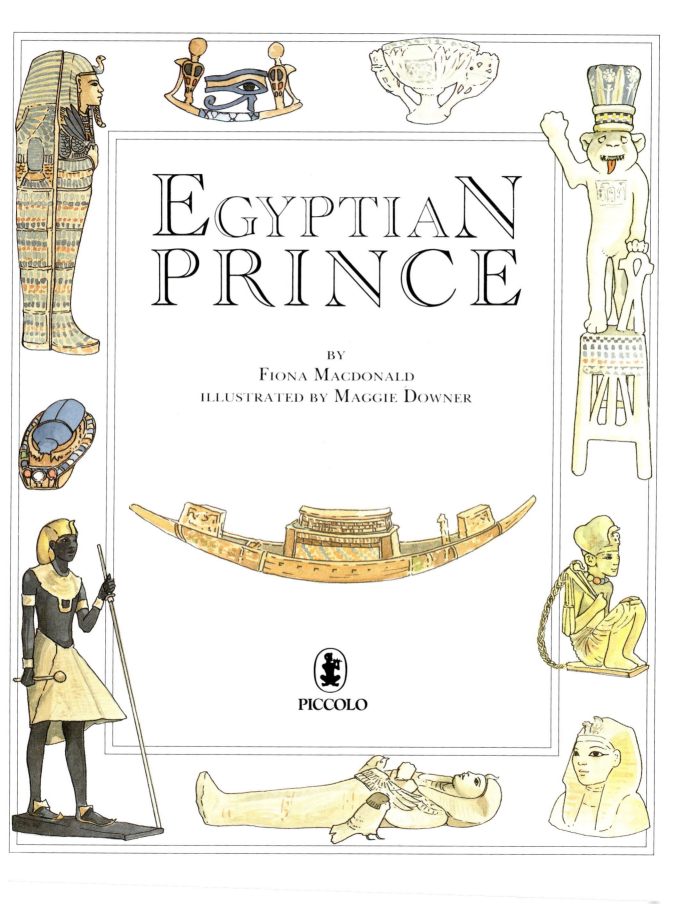

EGYPTIAN PRINCE

BY
FIONA MACDONALD
ILLUSTRATED BY MAGGIE DOWNER

PICCOLO

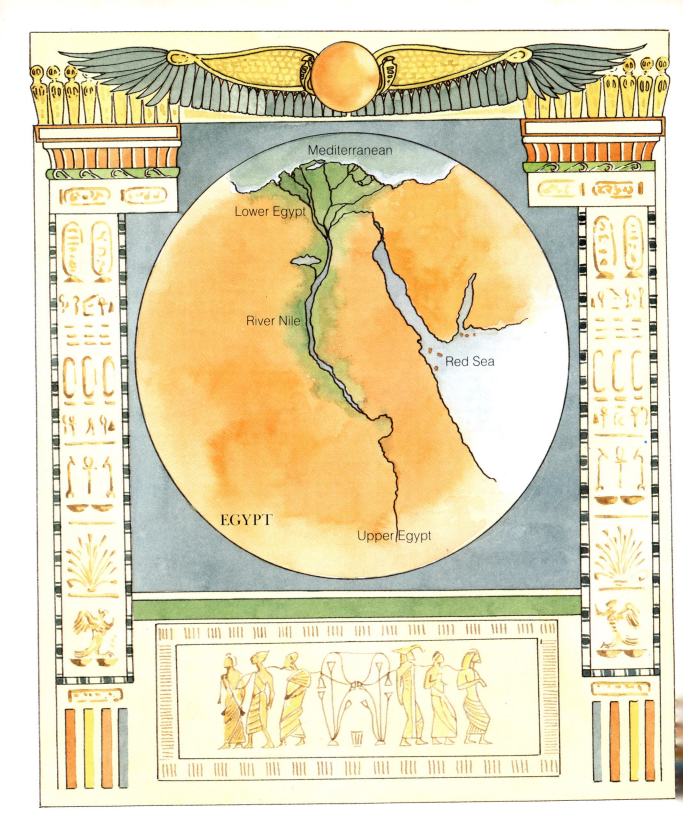

INTRODUCTION

Tutankhamun was a royal prince who lived in Egypt almost 3500 years ago. Archaeologists think that Tutankhamun was born in 1340 *BC*, and that he died in 1323 *BC*, when he was just seventeen years old. However, no documents have survived to tell us exactly when Tutankhamun lived.

There are many things that we do not know about Tutankhamun. But Tutankhamun's grave, which had remained lost for centuries and was rediscovered in 1922, has provided us with a great deal of information. It has helped us to find out about the skills, customs and beliefs of people who lived in Ancient Egypt.

Tutankhamun's life was tragically short. But for several years he was the most important person in Egypt. When he was about seven, Tutankhamun was crowned Pharaoh (supreme ruler) of his country. In this book, we will look at what life was like in Tutankhamun's vast and powerful kingdom.

THE RIVER KINGDOM

Egypt is a large country in north-eastern Africa. It is a very dry, desert land, where rain hardly ever falls. But the people who lived there in Tutankhamun's day were able to grow plentiful crops to feed themselves and their families. For thousands of years Egypt was the home of a splendid civilisation. How was this possible?

Egypt's wealth and prosperity was brought by the River Nile, one of the greatest rivers in the world. The Nile flows from the highlands of

A richly decorated royal boat gliding down the Nile. Great crowds gathered to watch a magnificent ship like this. They hoped to catch sight of the pharaoh, as well.

Ethiopia to the Mediterranean Sea. Every summer, the river became swollen with the rain that fell in the highlands. As a result, there were floods in Egypt. These floods brought water to make the crops grow, and spread fertile silt across the nearby fields.

The river-banks provided mud to make bricks, and reeds for paper-making. And the river was always busy with boats. Sailing down the Nile was the easiest way to travel through Tutankhamun's kingdom.

The Pharaoh was the most powerful man in Egypt. Beneath him in order of importance came priests, courtiers, merchants, craftsmen, farmers, labourers, and slaves.

Food was prepared and cooked by women and slaves. Grinding corn between two stones was hard work.

FOOD AND DRINK

Ordinary Egyptians living at this time ate simple food: bread, onions, lettuce, grapes and melons. Sometimes, they went hunting by the River Nile to catch wild ducks. Fish and water-fowl were trapped in nets thrown from boats, or speared as they swam in the shallows.

But normally, meat was only eaten by wealthy people. Archaeologists have found a carved frieze showing a pharaoh and his family feasting. They have the best of everything: lamb and goat roasted on skewers, morsels of duck, fine bread and cakes sweetened with honey, heaped platters of fruit decorated with flowers, wine and beer to drink.

Most Egyptians made their living from the land. They planted corn and vegetables in fields beside the river. Oxen were used for pulling carts and for ploughing. All the villagers helped to tend the new seedlings sprouting in the soft Nile mud. A good crop would mean plenty of food for everyone.

Wine was made from grapes. The juice was pressed by trampling the ripe grapes underfoot.

Tutankhamun's chair, used when he was a child, and buried in his tomb.

This footstool and splendid bed are from Tutankhamun's tomb.

Palaces for Pharaohs

The earliest rulers of Egypt built their palaces at Memphis, an important city in the north. But, by Tutankhamun's day, the pharaohs preferred to live in the magnificent city of Thebes, 500 kilometres further south. At Thebes, there were palaces, gardens, lakes filled by water channelled from the Nile, fine houses built for rich nobles, tall towers for storing grain, and a flourishing market with goods from many lands.

Palaces and houses were built of mud bricks, baked hard in the hot Egyptian sun. Frames for doors and windows were made of stone, and roofs were supported by graceful wooden columns. Wealthy homes had lavatories and showers, and were surrounded by a high wall, with a watchman always on guard. This is not surprising: like the royal palaces, they were filled with fine pottery, linens, and precious jewellery and exquisite furniture, decorated with ivory, ebony and, sometimes, thin layers of gold.

Going to School

Like other royal princes, Tutankhamun was probably sent to a school attached to a temple when he was only four years old. He spent the mornings there, learning how to read and write. In the afternoons – when it must have been very hot – he practised riding, wrestling and swimming. He also learned how to shoot with a bow and arrow. But what he really liked was going for walks with his dogs, or sitting in the shade with his friends playing "senet", a game like snakes and ladders.

Examples of hieroglyphs.

Board for playing "senet"; made of ebony and ivory.

The Egyptians wrote using picture-symbols, called hieroglyphs. Each hieroglyph stood for an object or an idea, and so words or sentences were made up of strings of little pictures, arranged in neat rows. Hieroglyphs were carved on statues and temple walls, or written very carefully on papyrus, using a miniature paintbrush made from chewed reeds. Ink was made from soot or finely ground red earth, mixed with gum. Mistakes were rubbed out with a piece of gritty stone, which was kept clean in a little leather bag.

Palette (flat, polished piece of ivory) for mixing inks. There is also a place to rest a reed-pen.

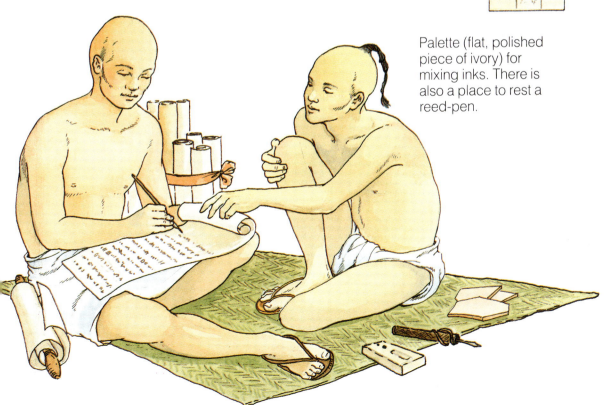

GODS AND RELIGION

The Egyptians believed in many gods. Some gods protected their homes and cities, others made their crops grow. There were river gods, gods of wind and weather, and sky gods. Some gods, like Horus, were shown as birds, others as cats and crocodiles. The most important was Amun, the "king of the gods".

Akenaten, the pharaoh who ruled before Tutankhamun, did not share

Ra   Isis   Osiris

Horus   Anubis   Hathor

his people's belief in all these gods. He also hated the wealth and power of Amun's priests. He believed that there was only one god, Aten (the Sun-disk), who brought peace and justice to the world. Akenaten built a whole new city dedicated to Aten, and composed hymns praising him.

But when Akenaten died, the old religion was brought back, and anyone who dared to mention Aten was punished. Even Tutankhamun had to obey this rule. He changed his name from Tutankhaten (as it originally was) to Tutankhamun. This showed that he was now a faithful worshipper of Amun.

Saying prayers in front of a sacred stone.

Markets

Egyptian artists and craft-workers were very skilful. They produced linen cloth, delicate pieces of jewellery, baskets woven from papyrus, fine furniture made from wood and leather, pottery, stone-carvings, glassware and weapons.

Market stalls in Egyptian cities were also well supplied with goods from distant lands. Merchants sold pottery from Syria and Greece, and oxen and slaves from Nubia. Cedarwood came from Lebanon, precious stones from Asia and India. All these goods were carried by river and unloaded at the busy

Goods on sale in the Egyptian market. The merchants and their customers are shaded from the hot sun by cloths stretched overhead.

docks. Grain and fresh vegetables were ferried by boat from villages along the river-bank.

The pharaohs loved gold, ebony, ivory, perfumes and spices. These were sent as tribute by peoples whom the Egyptian armies had conquered. Rich gifts were also exchanged with other rulers. The king of Assyria complained to Tutankhamun that he had sent a present of jewels and war-horses, but had received nothing in return.

CHILD OF THE GODS

As pharaoh, Tutankhamun was more than just a mighty ruler. He was also a priest, and, some people believed, the child of the gods. This meant that he had many religious duties to perform. He had to take part in ceremonies at the temples, say prayers and make offerings to the gods so that earlier pharaohs, now dead, would not be forgotten.

Earrings belonging to Tutankhamun

Part of a necklace from Tutankhamun's tomb; made of gold, glass and precious stones.

The most splendid religious festival was the Feast of Opet. It took place once a year, at the time of the Nile floods. Majestic statues of the god Amun and his wife were loaded on to a barge. With Tutankhamun's own royal boat leading the way, they were rowed up the river, so that everyone could see them.

Crowds gathered on the river-banks to watch the Opet procession. People wore their best clothes and jewellery. Once the procession had passed by, the rest of the day was spent in feasting and fun. Musicians and acrobats danced in the streets.

Tombs and Treasures

We know so much about life in Tutankhamun's Egypt because of the thousands of wonderful objects preserved in his tomb. All the Egyptian pharaohs – and anyone else who could afford it – were buried in large, costly tombs, but most of these have been robbed or destroyed. Some have been lost for ever beneath the desert sands.

Plan of Tutankhamun's tomb

Why did the Egyptians spend so much time and money building beautiful tombs for themselves and

Workmen decorating a tomb with paintings and carvings.

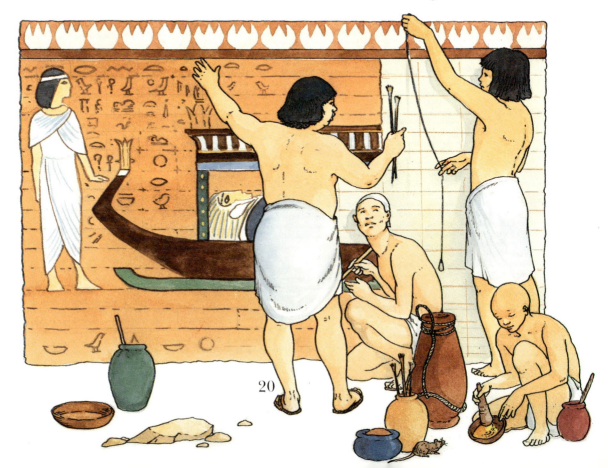

their families? They believed that these tombs would be their "eternal homes". They thought that their souls would survive only while their bodies were safely preserved. And so they built strong, secure tombs, where their bodies could rest.

Tombs were so important that they were built while the person who was going to be buried in them was still alive. In time, vast "cities of the dead" were created. The most famous of these is called the Valley of the Kings and is on the opposite bank of the river from Thebes, the pharaohs' capital.

1. Small coffin.
2. Shrine
3. Tutankhamun's funeral mask made of gold.

Mummies

Egyptian mortuary workers developed some skilful ways of preserving dead bodies from decay. They turned them into mummies – dried, and shrivelled dead bodies, tightly bandaged with white linen.

How was a mummy made? First of all, the brain, heart, lungs, liver, stomach and intestines were taken from the body. (To be preserved separately, in special jars with tight fitting lids.) Then the whole body was washed with herbal oils, to kill any germs, and placed in a tub of "natron", a chemical which absorbs moisture. It was left there for about forty days. Then it was smeared with more herbal oils, and wrapped tightly in linen bandages.

The finished mummy was packed into a stone chest (a "sarcophagus") or a wooden coffin and buried in a chamber, usually underground. The hot, dry air of Egypt helped to preserve the body. Thousands of mummies have survived and can be seen in museums around the world.

Tutankhamun's mummy was surrounded by three golden burial chests.

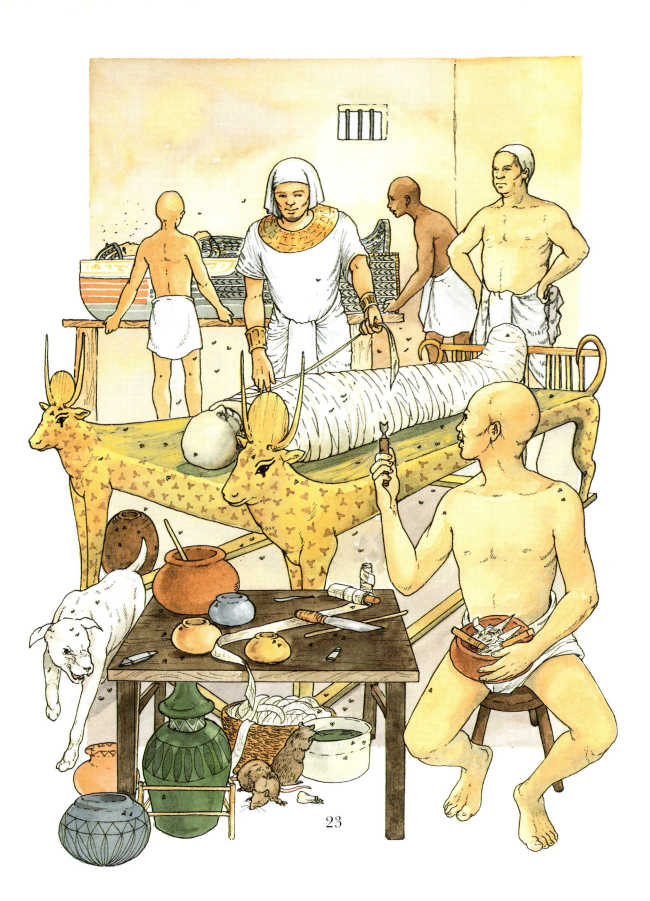

LIFE AFTER DEATH

The funeral ceremonies for a pharaoh like Tutankhamun were very elaborate. Prayers and rituals lasted for several days.

Tutankhamun's grave was painted with scenes of him taking part in all kinds of activities – hunting, fighting, eating, and relaxing with his wife. For the Egyptians, these paintings had magic powers. They made sure that Tutankhamun would go on to lead the same sort of life after death as he did when alive.

Many of the objects buried alongside Tutankhamun are made of gold because gold lasts for ever.

Before Tutankhamun's mummy was finally buried in his tomb, his relations said prayers and made offerings to the gods.

Tutankhamun's tomb was also filled with precious objects. Some, like the jewellery and clothing, belonged to him when he was alive. He would need them after death. Others, like the weapons and chariots, were there to help him fight against the shadowy creatures he would meet in the kingdom of the dead. It was believed that if Tutankhamun survived these battles, he would be united with the gods, and be reborn. His spirit would live again in the bodies of the pharaohs who ruled after him.

Time Chart

Egypt and Middle East

c 2000 BC	Rise of the Hittite empire in Turkey and surrounding lands.
c 1750 BC	Hammurabi founds great empire based in Babylon (Iraq).
1640 BC	Hyksos people invade Egypt.
c 1567–1089 BC	Period known as the 'New Kingdom' in Egypt, after Pharaohs drive out invading Hyksos peoples and take control.
c 1370 BC	Pharaoh Akenaton introduces new religion worshipping the sun-disk and starts to build new capital city.
c 1340–1323 BC	Tutankhamun's lifespan.
c 1200 BC	Jewish people led by the Prophet Moses leave Egypt (where they had been living) and set up new kingdom in Palestine.
c 1166 BC	Death of Ramesses III, last great pharaoh of Egypt.

America and the Pacific

c 2000–c 1000 BC	Indonesian peoples settle throughout the Melanesian Islands in the Pacific Ocean.
c 2000–1000 BC	Settled farming spreads throughout Central America. Maize is ground in special stone bowls, known as 'metates'.
c 2000 BC onwards	American potters, especially in Mexico and Guatemala, make fine statues and other pottery. In Ecuador, finely-decorated containers are made out of dried fruit (gourds).
c 2000 BC	Beginnings of metal-working in Peru. Cloth is also made.
c 1800 BC	Great religious centre built at Kotosh (Peru) on terraces built of huge stone blocks.
c 1300 BC	Pacific Ocean migrants reach Fiji and establish new civilisation there.
c 1150 BC	Beginnings of powerful Olmec empire, based in Mexico.

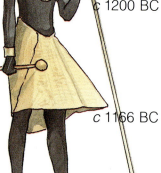

EUROPE		ASIA AND AFRICA	
c 2000 BC	Stonehenge (southern England) built.	*c* 2500 BC onwards	Sahara desert begins to expand, turning fertile regions of North Africa into empty desert.
c 2000-1000 BC	Bronze-working skills develop throughout Europe. Rock-pictures of religious and hunting scenes found at sites in Italy and Scandinavia. Tribes led by warrior chiefs rule over scattered kingdoms.	*c* 2000-1000 BC	Settled farming becomes more widespread south of the Sahara
		c 1600 BC	The rise of Shang civilisation in China. Growth of towns and production of beautiful bronze objects.
c 2000-1450 BC	Splendid Minoan civilisation flourishes on island of Crete.	*c* 1550 BC	Aryan invaders attack India and destroy 'Indus Valley' civilisation.
c 1600-1200 BC	Mycenean civilisation powerful in Greece.	*c* 1500 BC	Chinese invent picture-script (the basis of present-day Chinese writing). Beautiful silk cloth woven.
c 1500 BC	Greeks and Minoans develop a form of writing known as 'linear B script'.		
c 1250 BC	Period of the 'Trojan Wars' between Greece and kingdoms in Turkey.	*c* 1450 BC	Beginning of Indian Hindu religion (worship of Brahma).
c 1100 BC	Phoenecian traders in the Mediterranean become increasingly powerful. They develop the first alphabet-based writing.	*c* 1027 BC	Shang rulers in China overthrown by Chou peoples. Farming develops.
c 1000 BC	Rise of Etruscan civilisation in Italy.	*c* 900 BC	Rise of Kingdom of Kush (now Sudan).

Word List

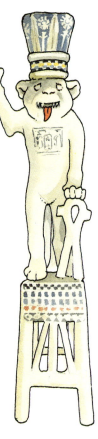

Absorbs Soaks up.

Archaeologists People who study the remains of past civilisations.

Barge A long, flat, narrow boat.

Capital The most important. A capital city is usually where the king or queen of a country lives.

Cedarwood Sweet-smelling wood from the cedar tree, used in important buildings and to make boxes and fine furniture. Cedarwood also protects cloth from being eaten by insects.

Ceremonies Special actions, which often included some hymns, some prayers and processions, to mark important occasions.

Chamber A small room.

Channelled Made to flow in a particular direction.

Civilisation How a particular group of people live. What they believe, how they work and what their houses, cities and works of art are like. For example, historians write about "Egyptian civilisation".

Columns Tall thin posts used to hold up a roof or another part of a building.

Customs Ways of doing things.

Dedicated Given specially to, or built specially for.

Documents Writings on paper or a similar substance, like papyrus (see below). Historians have discovered a great deal of information about past civilisations by studying old documents.

Ebony A precious, hard, shiny black wood from a tree that grows in Africa.

Elaborate Complicated

Exquisite Fine and delicate.

Fertile Good for growing crops.

Frieze A long, narrow picture, often telling a story, rather like a comic-strip today. Friezes were used to decorate buildings and tombs in ancient Egypt.

Grave The place where a dead person is buried.

Gritty Rough. Made up of lots of tiny, sharp pieces.

Ground Broken up into a fine powder.

Herbal Made from herbs.

Image Picture.

28

Intestines Long "tubes" inside the human body where food is processed after leaving the stomach.

Ivory A precious, smooth, shiny white substance, made from elephant tusks (large front teeth).

Linen A type of cloth made from flax, a plant that grows in marshy ground. The land beside the River Nile was ideal for growing flax. The Egyptians wore clothes made of linen cloth, which is cool and comfortable in hot weather.

Morsels Little pieces.

Oxen Large animals, rather like cows.

Papyrus A type of 'paper' made from reeds which grew beside the River Nile.

Pharaoh The ruler of Egypt. The pharaoh was very powerful; he was feared and worshipped by many of the people that he ruled. He was almost like a god.

Platters Large flat dishes.

Plentiful Lots of.

Preserved Kept safe and free from decay.

Prosperity Being rich; with plenty of food, goods and money.

Reeds A plant like tall, thick grass, which grows beside rivers. Papyrus (see above) is a type of reed.

Ritual A series of actions which are designed to please the gods, or to help someone who has died. Saying prayers and singing hymns are one type of ritual.

Rushes Another grass-like plant (see reeds, above) which grows in marshy land beside rivers.

Seedlings Young, fragile plants, which have just sprouted from seeds planted in the earth.

Shallows Places where the water is not very deep.

Shrivelled Shrunken.

Skewers Long, thin spears, made of wood or metal. Pieces of meat can be threaded on skewers and cooked over a fire.

Silt Fine, soft, sticky earth, left by rivers after floods. Silt is a very good soil for growing crops.

Sun-disk the god of the morning sun in the form of a winged beetle.

Supreme most important and powerful.

Tomb A building (can be underground) where a dead person is buried.

Tribute A kind of forced present from a conquered people to their rulers.

Water-fowl Birds, such as ducks and geese, that live on or near water.

INDEX

NOTE: References to illustrations are in bold

A

Akenaten, King of Egypt 14–15
Amun (god) 14, 15, 18
Aten (god) 15

B

boats **6,** 7
bodies, preservation of 21, 22
bricks 7, 10

C

cedarwood 16, 28
crops 6, 7, 8

E

Egypt 6

F

feasts 18, **19**
fish 8
floods 7
friezes 8, 28
funeral ceremonies 24
furniture 10, **10,** 16

G

gifts, from pharaohs 17
gods 14–15, 18
gold 25

H

hieroglyphs **12,** 13
homes, of the wealthy 10
Horus (god) 14
hunting 8, **9**

I

ink 13

J

jewellery 16, 18, **18**

L

linen 16, 29

M

markets 16–17, **16–17**
meat 8
Memphis 10
merchants 16
mummies 22, **23**

N

Nile River 6/7, 16

O

Opet, feast of 18
oxen 8, 16

P

paintings 24
palaces 10
papyrus 13, 29
pharaohs 7, 8, 10, 17
priests 18

R

reeds 7, 29
religious festivals 18

S

schools 12
sculptures **14**
senet 12, **12**
slaves 16
Sun-disk 15, 29

T

Thebes 10
tombs 20–1
Tutankhamun, King of Egypt 6, 12, 15, 17
    furniture of **10**
    jewellery of **18**
    tomb of 24–25

V

Valley of the Kings 21

W

wine 8
writing 13

Notes for Teachers on History in the National Curriculum

The new National Curriculum for History, which lays down a prescribed course of study for pupils aged five to fourteen plus, was introduced into schools in England and Wales during the autumn term 1991.

This series of books has been designed to provide background information relevant to the designated Core History Study Units for Key Stage 2 (i.e., for pupils aged seven to eleven), and also to the Optional History Study Units at the same Key Stage level. Younger children, in particular, should find the short, simple text and largely visual presentation of information appropriate to their needs.

This volume in the series, *Egyptian Prince*, relates in particular to the Supplementary Study Unit "Ancient Egypt" listed under Category C of the final government document "History in the National Curriculum (England)", published by HMSO in March 1991. As from that date, pupils are now required to study at least one topic from this category, in addition to the compulsory Core Units, and, for a variety of reasons, the study of Ancient Egypt must rank as one of the most immediately appealing of all the options listed.

Further, non-statutory guidance on the preferred content of these optional study units has yet to be issued as this book goes to press, but it is worth noting that, in earlier government publications* relating to History in the National Curriculum, the study of Ancient Egypt was commended as "widening perspectives". Topics then recommended for study included:

Pharaohs in Egypt
Irrigation and agriculture of the Nile delta as a basis of
    Egyptian civilisation.
Everyday life
Slavery
Egyptian art - friezes
Egypt: divine rulers. Codified laws. Tutankhamun
Egypt: priests, officials, scribes, peasants, slaves
Egyptian religious practices, afterlife, mummies, tombs
Egyptian carving, painting, elaborate tombs, grave goods

All are covered in this book.

* National Curriculum History Working Group's Final Report (HMSO, April 1990, p 44).

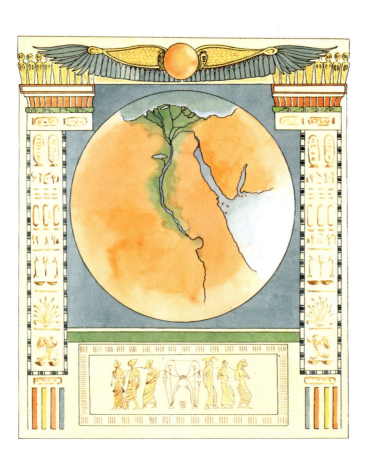